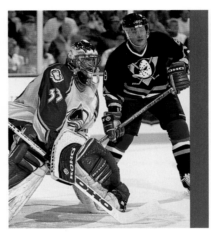 

HOCKEY THE NHL® WAY
Power Plays
and Penalty Killing

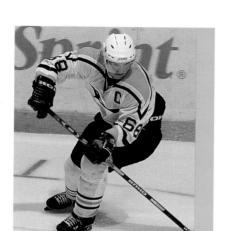
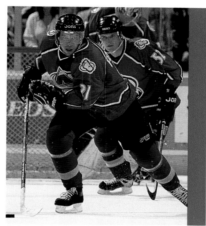
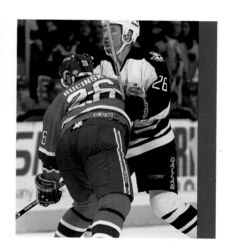

Sean Rossiter &
Paul Carson

GREYSTONE BOOKS
Douglas & McIntyre Publishing Group
Vancouver/Toronto/New York

BUTLER ACRES LIBRARY

To Jan, Tamera and Kellin, who continue to inspire and encourage me. — PAUL CARSON

Copyright © 2000 by Sean Rossiter

00 01 02 03 04 5 4 3 2 1

Greystone Books
A division of Douglas & McIntyre Ltd.
2323 Quebec Street, Suite 201
Vancouver, British Columbia
Canada V5T 4S7

Canadian Cataloguing in Publication Data
Rossiter, Sean, 1946 –
    Power plays and penalty killing
    (Hockey the NHL way)
    ISBN 1-55054-791-7

    1. Hockey—Offense—Juvenile literature. Hockey—Defense—Juvenile literature.
I. Carson, Paul, 1955– II. Title. III. Series
GV847.25.R67 2000   j796.962'2   C00-910385-6

Editing by Anne Rose and Kerry Banks
Cover and text design by Peter Cocking
Instructional photographs: Stefan Schulhof/Schulhof Photography
Front cover photograph: *Petr Nedved & Wade Redden* by Bruce Bennett/
    Bruce Bennett Studios
Back cover photographs by Bruce Bennett Studios. Photographers:
    Pavel Bure: Jim McIsaac • *Patrick Roy & Teemu Selanne:* John Giamundo •
    Mark Recchi: Jim Leary • *Jaromir Jagr:* Dennis Clark • *Peter Forsberg,*
    Martin Rucinsky & Jere Lehtinen: Bruce Bennett
Printed and bound in Canada by Friesens
Printed on acid-free paper ∞

The publisher gratefully acknowledges the assistance of the Canada Council and of the British Columbia Ministry of Tourism, Small Business and Culture. The publisher also acknowledges the financial support of the Government of Canada through the Book Publishing Industry Development Program (BPIDP) for its publishing activities.

Contents

The NHL Way team

Our players

Tyler Hansen   Derek MacKenzie   Shayne Russell   David Mercer

Shae Dehaan   Dane Stevens   Brooks Stillie   Luke Holowaty

Tory Malinoski   Kellin Carson   Jaysen Mah   Lance Quan

Our NHL Way coach

Paul Carson, co-author
Coaching committee chair, the Canadian Hockey Association

An assistant coach with the UBC Thunderbirds for seven seasons, Paul Carson also served as the provincial coach coordinator responsible for coach development programs in B.C. for four years. Two years ago, Paul stepped down from his provincial coach job to accept a position with the CHA coaching committee. His coaching resume includes high school hockey in Japan, all levels of minor hockey and guest coaching roles in Great Britain and Europe. He was a guest speaker at the Molson Open Ice Summit in 1999 and has presented at numerous coaching clinics, seminars and conferences. He continues to work as an author of the very successful CHA Nike Skills series.

Special thanks

Special thanks, first and foremost, to the parents of the NHL Way players. Thanks also to Greg Stangel of NHL Enterprises and the NHL players who shared their secrets; to ace rink roadie Bob Kemmis; to the staff of the UBC Thunderbird Winter Sports Centre, who made us feel welcome; and to the staff at Cyclone Taylor Sporting Goods: Rick and Mark Taylor, and Mike Cox. Thanks as well to Rich Helmer, Ewart Blackmore, Jack James and Dave Merrell of the Vancouver Flames old-timers, for the faceoff clinic.

Powerful and fast, Mats Sundin is at home along the boards or in the slot. He can do the dirty work, make plays or finish around the net with his soft hands and scoring touch.

Foreword

Hockey is a tough sport. It is played with sticks, sharp skate-blades, an ice surface hard as concrete and boards that can rattle your bones. The rules of hockey are there to make the game as safe as possible, so the price for breaking them is high. No other major team sport punishes every personal foul by removing the offender from play—for two minutes, five minutes, 10 minutes, or the entire game.

When a penalty is called by the referee and the offending player is sent to the penalty box, the offender's team must play shorthanded for as long as the penalty lasts or until a goal is scored. These players are known as the penalty-killing unit, or, as many coaches call them, the PK. Their opponents are on a power play, or PP. Both units are often called special teams.

The power play is a game within a game. It is hockey at its most intense. Power plays often decide the outcomes of games. A well-run power play gives a team a one-in-four chance to score. But having one or two more players on the ice than your opponents does not mean your team *will* score. To do that, your power play needs a solid plan. *Hockey the NHL Way: Power Plays and Penalty Killing* shows you how to turn those extra players into goals.

We also know that good teams in the National Hockey League are able to kill off nine out of every 10 penalties. Nothing changes the momentum of a game like killing off a penalty. One moment the team with a player in the box is in big trouble; the next moment that team has new life.

No wonder a team's power-play and penalty-killing units are often called special teams. To be a special player, you have to be on the ice when the game is on the line.

Every coach looks for the kind of players who appear in *Hockey the NHL Way: Power Plays and Penalty Killing*: smart players, two-way players, players who skate hard and play as a team. The kind of player *you* can be.

Marc Crawford
Head coach, the Vancouver Canucks

Introduction

Power plays and penalty killing are a big part of hockey, but until now there have been no books that advise young players, or coaches, on what to do when a player goes to the penalty box—even though it often happens 10 times in a game. That's nearly a dozen times (or almost half an hour) during a game when players on the ice must adjust to having more, or fewer, players than their opponents. When that happens, it's a whole new game.

Now, *Hockey the NHL Way: Power Plays and Penalty Killing* shows you what's going on when someone is in the box, and how to play on the power-play or penalty-killing units. Full-page colour photos of NHL stars in action, with tips from the best players in the game, show you how it's done.

One of the surprises in this book is that power plays and penalty killing have more in common than you might think. It takes special players to play on special teams. Players who can check or protect the puck. Players who skate hard both ways. Players who like to prevent goals as much as score them.

Finally, in both situations, you have to read-and-react when puck possession changes from one team to the other. When the penalty-killing unit gets the puck, it goes on offense. When that happens, the players on the power-play unit have to switch quickly to defense. Players on special teams have to be ready to change roles in an instant.

Sometimes on special teams it's the little things that make the difference. Faceoffs, for example, are even more important during penalties. Learn what you should be trying to do on faceoffs, depending on where they happen and whether your team has more or less players than usual.

Another unique feature of *Hockey the NHL Way: Power Plays and Penalty Killing* are the tips on goaltending. Everyone knows how important the goalie is in killing off a penalty. But not every goalie or coach is fully aware of every aspect of the goaltender's role on the power play.

Mark Recchi is an explosive two-way special teams player, who scores about 10 power-play goals a season and attacks point men on the penalty kill.

You don't have to be the smoothest player on your club to get power-play minutes. But you do have to be useful.

It helps to be good with the puck. You must be able to make and receive passes. That means more than having good hands. It means being able to see the ice around you—to read-and-react. And it means being able to protect the puck. Passing and protecting the puck are basic hockey skills.

On the power play, coaches look for players who want to compete. You want to make plays. You want the puck. You want to take the shot. You want to go to the net.

Is that you?

SPECIAL

TEAMS

Eric Lindros uses a stick with a firm shaft and a nearly straight blade—better for faceoffs and backhand shots, like this one.

Maybe your team has the extra attacker, or maybe this time your team is killing a penalty. Either way, it's the same game. You are still playing hockey. Here's what to focus on.

Pressure your opponents

Always *pressure* the other team. On the power play or the penalty kill, that means using your speed. It means moving the puck if you have it or being in position to get it. It means daring your opponents to take the puck away. You have to compete. As Pavel Bure says, "Be a player."

Support your teammates

Always give *support* to your teammates. On the power play, support means getting free and being ready to take a pass. On the penalty kill, support means picking up your check in the neutral

A good way into the penalty-kill box is with a give-and-go pass to a teammate in close support...

...After passing, move into the open lane for a return pass.

Attack

zone and blocking a passing lane in your own zone. Hockey is still a team game, and never more so than with someone in the penalty box.

Make transitions

Hockey is a *transition* game. That's trans-i-shun, and it means change. When your team gets the puck you are on offense. When your team loses it, you are a defender. Read what's happening, and react to it. Be a two-way player.

The basics

You know that there are differences between power plays and penalty killing. One difference is the number of players you have on the ice. But it's more important to know how power plays and penalty killing are the same. The key point to remember is that penalty-killing and power-play units both work with time and space; they just use them in different ways.

On the power play

The power-play unit has a certain amount of time to work with, plus a little more space than when the sides are even. On a power play you need to use that time and space to try and score. The idea is to get the puck into the middle of your opponents' zone—the shooting zone—and take your shot.

After passing, the forward on the boards creates pressure by moving into the slot for a return pass . . .

. . . while, inside the penalty-kill box, the original puck carrier takes the return pass.

Penalty killing

Penalty killers work with time, too. They are trying to *stall* and *contain:* to hold things up. First, you forecheck, to keep the power-play unit in its defensive zone and contain it there, if possible. Once the power-play unit is set up in your zone, your penalty-killing unit will try to push the power play to the outside. On a penalty kill, your job is to keep the power-play unit out of the shooting zone. Then, once you get the puck, you can make the power-play unit chase *you.*

"On the penalty kill you can use your speed. The other team can try so hard to score that they take risks with their passes, creating a breakdown and a short-handed scoring chance."

JEFF FRIESEN

Before the whistle

A key part of many power plays is the short period of time before the referee blows the whistle to stop play and send the offender to the penalty box. The idea is to give the good guys a chance to score even before the offender gets the gate. This is called a "delayed penalty."

Most penalties happen when defenders are under pressure near their own net. Almost always the attackers have the puck when a penalty is called. The referee will signal that a penalty will be called by raising his arm, but then delays blowing the whistle as long as the team that did not commit the penalty controls the puck. The whistle blows when the penalized team touches the puck.

Delayed penalties

By spotting the referee's raised arm, the goalie can leave the ice in favour of an extra attacker.

. . . and when you are sure your team's been fouled, turn on the jets. Take short, choppy strides.

What to do

The clock does not start running on a penalty until the referee blows play to a stop. Often the defenders are mixed up and running around, so the best time to score is usually *before* the whistle blows. That time lasts as long as the non-penalized team can keep the puck. As long as the team that will go on the power play can keep the puck, it can add an attacker and actually add time to the penalty!

When the referee has his or her arm up and your team has the puck, you know you are going on the power play.

For a brief moment, while the referee delays calling the penalty, the attacking team can replace its goalie with an extra attacker. To get the extra attacker on the ice, two players must see the referee's arm signal. Your goaltender must see it and skate to the bench. (The team that is about to be penalized can not score; as soon as they get the puck, the whistle will sound.) The other player who must notice the referee's signal is the one who will replace the goalie on the ice. That player is usually the centre of the line going on the ice for the next shift.

Delayed penalties checklist

■ First, your goaltender must get to the bench. If you see a penalty about to be called but your goalie hasn't noticed, call your

Here, the bench is ready. Shout "Next centre!" as you get close.

The sixth attacker is off and running. Get your power play off to a great start.

A sharp goalie gives his team a lift by getting to the bench fast.

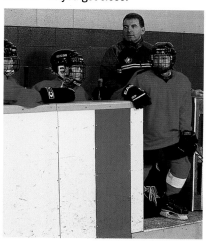

Delayed penalties

goalie to the bench. When the goalie is within 10 feet/3 m of the bench, the extra attacker can go over the boards.

■ One way to keep possession is to pass the puck to your point, who may decide to bring the puck back into the neutral zone. If that happens, it is important for those teammates on the ice to get back and give support to the puck carrier.

■ Don't just stand around and celebrate when the referee is about to call a penalty against your opponents. There are things you can do to help your team score—*before* the ref blows the whistle.

The trick to a successful power play is to make the best use of the extra players on the ice. The idea is to get a shot from the ideal scoring position—right in front of your opponents' net. With the advantage of one or more players, your power-play unit should be able to do that.

A top NHL power-play unit scores on just one in four chances; the best NHL penalty-killing units keep their opponents from scoring nine out of 10 times. So it is easier to kill a penalty than to score on the power play. This means that for your team to score, your power play needs a plan of attack. A good power play is not just more players, it is more players with a plan.

POWER

PLAYS

Getting the puck into the offensive zone

Most penalties are called on defenders, so power plays usually begin in the offensive zone. But, because penalty killers are allowed to ice the puck, many power-play scoring chances begin with players breaking out of their own zone. This means that the first thing to do on a power play is to get the puck into the offensive zone and control it there if necessary.

How to do it

There are three ways you can bring the puck into the offensive zone: carry the puck in; chip the puck off the boards; or dump-and-chase. All three plays are easy—and effective. Remember: which play you choose depends on what you see at the blueline.

The offensive zone

Carry the puck until you are checked. Don't pass until you have to. Get the puck deep . . .

. . . then make the pass to an open teammate. Remember: if you are being checked, somebody's open.

Carry the puck in

The best way to get the puck into the offensive zone is to carry it in—skate the puck through the neutral zone until you are pressured. Your aim in getting the puck deep is to buy your teammates time to set up the power play. Once inside the offensive zone, there are a few good ways to get the puck to a teammate.

Pass to an open teammate: If you are crossing the blueline close to the boards, skate hard with the puck and make a sharp turn toward the boards. That should shake off any checker. Next, look to pass to a teammate deeper in the zone. If there is no one open, look to the near-side point.

Pass behind the net: If you have moved deep into the offensive zone and find yourself being double-teamed, pass behind the net off the end-boards to a teammate on the other side. If you are under pressure, chances are a teammate is free on the other side of the ice.

Chip the puck off the boards

Your second option is to chip the puck off the boards past the defensive pressure. A teammate skating close to you can skate onto the loose puck and gain control deep in the zone.

The open teammate is often on the other side of the zone. Off the boards behind the penalty-killing team's net is a good idea.

The offensive zone

Remember:
- Carry the puck until checked. If there is no pressure, go all the way to the net.
- Move up the ice as a unit. Support the puck carrier by being available for a pass.
- Never go offside on a power play. There's plenty of time.
- Once in the zone, you *want* defenders to attack you. This opens up passing lanes.
- Be aggressive. Be in control.

Dump-and-chase

Sometimes penalty killers line up along their blueline, making it hard to carry the puck into their zone. When this happens, the best way to get the puck into their zone is to dump-and-chase. Make sure you are past the red centre-ice line. Flip the puck high and deep, then skate hard after it. The penalty killers have to turn around and get going, and may be slow getting to the puck; you and your teammates should beat them to the puck.

Offensive zone checklist

- Read-and-react to what you see as you move through the neutral zone.
- Choose the right play (you have three choices) to get the puck into the offensive zone.

Dump the puck

When your opponents are guarding their blueline, dump the puck. Shoot after you cross the centre-ice line . . .

. . . The winger on the other side must beat the defenseman to the puck and control it.

T I P
One way to keep the puck away from your opponents' goalie is to dump it into a corner.

- Pressure the defensive team by skating hard into the zone, attracting checkers.
- Remember that if the team with the extra attacker can't get set up in the offensive zone, there is no power play. (A power-play unit will sometimes score on the rush. But a power-play unit is usually set up to match a penalty-killing unit player for player, and to outnumber them in a certain area: near the net, in the slot or in the shooting zone.)

"I try to learn something every day. You get more experience; you become an older, smarter player. You try to run around less and play more with your brains."

PAVEL BURE

The key power-play skill you need is the ability to see the ice and put the puck on the stick of the player most likely to score. That is a rare skill, even in the NHL. It is so rare that players who can fill that role are called power-play quarterbacks. One reason they are called that is because a successful power play usually requires set plays—planned out before the game, as in football. In football, most plays start with the quarterback handling the ball. In hockey, a good power play works the same way.

There are four key steps to most power plays:

1. Control and protect the puck.
2. Move the puck.
3. Get into the box.
4. Work the plan.

Master all four steps and you'll be a power-play quarterback.

Quarterback the PP

This is Kellin Carson quarterbacking the power play, but it could be Paul Kariya . . .

. . . and with the puck controlled by the power-play unit, the next step is to get it to the point. Here, Kellin looks to the far post and his open teammate.

Control and protect the puck

If the puck is *carried* over the blueline, your teammates must:

- Stay open and close by for quick, short passes.

If the puck is *dumped* in, your teammates must:

- Skate hard to the puck.
- Outnumber the defenders at the puck.
- Move the puck to the point. Or, if they can't move the puck,
- Protect the puck and wait for help.

"If you don't have a good power play, or at least an average power play, you're not going to win many games."

PAUL KARIYA

"All that is going through my mind in a power-play faceoff is to try and move the puck back. The longer you have the puck on the power play, the better."

MIKE MODANO

Use your teammates

On the power play, the puck carrier must pressure the defenders by moving the puck. To do that, the puck carrier must see open teammates. Each offensive player must:

- Provide a passing option for the puck carrier. Every pass means your team might lose the puck, so passes should be short, crisp, and stick-to-stick.
- Work to offer a pass-receiving option. Beat your check.
- Adjust and offer close support when a teammate receives the puck. (On receiving the puck, the new puck carrier must protect it. Move to give support by being ready to receive the next pass.)

T I P

If you keep the puck moving it changes the point of attack—forcing players on a penalty kill to chase the puck.

Move the puck quickly, and know what you are going to do with it before it comes to you.

Teammates must move between penalty killers to create options for the puck carrier. Here, Dane Stevens makes the right choice—to pass.

Move the puck

Power-play checklist

- The breakout from your own zone must be smooth and according to plan, with players moving up the ice together.
- Movement through the neutral zone must be as a five-player unit to keep each penalty killer busy.
- Keep or gain control of the puck in the offensive zone.
- After the power play is set up in the offensive zone, play as a unit.
- Each player must move into the open spaces to create passing lanes for the puck carrier.

Walkout lanes

A penalty-killing unit on a five-on-four must protect the shooting zone by forming a box. Your power-play unit must attack the box by moving the puck inside the box where the chances of scoring are high. A good way to do this is by moving into the box through the openings between defenders. On a five-on-four power play, there are five gaps between defenders, one for each power-play attacker. These are called "walkout lanes."

Two teammates, one with the puck, form a two-on-one against one defender. Either attacker can pressure the box by forcing the defender to make a choice. In committing to either attacker, the defender opens up a walkout lane, making it bigger. As the puck carrier, you read-and-react to the defender's choice, passing or keeping the puck. Either way, the puck moves into the box.

Get into the box

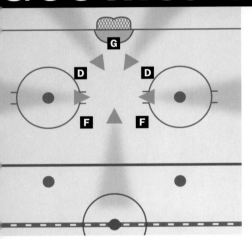

The openings between penalty killers in their box are called the "walkout lanes."

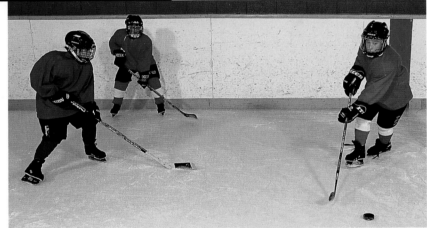

The point man moves the puck into the middle of the ice, trying to get to the shooting lane before the defender.

Creating pressure

As a puck carrier and offensive player, you can enter these lanes to create pressure in front of the net—in two ways:
■ You can carry the puck into the box. Or,
■ You can pass the puck to a teammate and move into the lane for a return pass. This creates a two-on-one against the nearest defender. Play this situation as you would any two-on-one, by reading-and-reacting to the choices the defender must make.

Most power-play set-ups occur at the half-boards, near the outside of the faceoff circles. Usually, this is where the power-play quarterback will be. That's because there are so many passing options from this spot. From here, as the power-play quarterback you have several options to choose from:

- If your teammate in the middle is available, that's your first choice.
- Passing to the point is a safe choice that moves the puck toward the middle.
- Passing to the low forward puts pressure on the strong-side defenseman. (The strong side is the side where the puck is.) It also opens up your chance of another pass, into the slot.
- Or you could move toward the blueline, move down low, or try to carry the puck into the slot and see if a defender will bite.

N H L   T I P

"If the penalty killers contract down to the net area, you can sneak in from the point. If some guy misreads the play and goes the wrong way, go to the net."
D A R R Y L   S Y D O R

Always be ready to shoot on the point. Here, the defender over-plays the passer, so Kellin is open to shoot . . .

. . . To give himself a better shooting angle, he drags the puck into the middle. He can now shoot toward the net.

Work the plan

Read-and-react

Which play you should make depends on what the two defenders on your side of the box are doing. If one of the defenders moves toward you, the quarterback, you could direct the puck to the area the defender just left, to take advantage of that open space.

By passing the puck and moving into the slot for a return pass, you force the defender to make a choice. As in a two-on-one, you or your teammate will be open to take the pass and shoot.

Setting it up

Most goals scored on the power play start from point shots. Here are two simple plays to set up the point shooter.

Move to the middle and shoot

The power-play quarterback passes to the near, or strong-side, point. The point shooter moves to the middle of the ice and shoots. Both the low forward and the quarterback enter the box to look for a rebound. If the defender at the top of the box moves along the blueline with the point shooter, the quarterback is open and should get a return pass from the point.

The point shot

A point shooter must make quick choices. Pass or shoot? This defender is off his line to the net . . .

. . . so he shoots. Shooting low makes the goalie handle the shot with his or her stick. Rebounds are more likely.

NHL TIP

"I'm just trying to get my power-play point shot on the net. I want to get it past the defender trying to block it, or to my teammates in front of the net for a deflection."

WADE REDDEN

The one-timer

Instead of shooting, the strong-side defenseman takes the pass and moves the puck to his or her partner for a one-timer shot. The pass should arrive just ahead of the receiver, and on the ice.

As a point shooter you always have the option of shooting to the side of the low forward for the easy tip-in. All your point shots should be low to create rebounds. As Wade Redden says, "The one thing you don't want to do is miss the far post—the puck will hit the boards and go around the zone."

Remember: If your shot line to the net is blocked, get the puck deep along the boards. A blocked point shot can result in a breakaway on your net.

Al MacInnis has the most feared point shot in the NHL. It enables him to take a little off his laser delivery to make his bullets tippable at the net—or to fake the shot and pass.

Many power plays begin with faceoffs in the offensive zone These might be the most important faceoffs of the entire game. All the basics of faceoffs apply in this case, and some are critical.

Learn from faceoffs against the same opponent early in the game. For example, how does the other centre grip the stick? Remember: As a centre you must make sure that each of your teammates is positioned in the correct spot before going to the dot. Take your time. Watch the official's hand. Have a plan.

Here are three ways to win a faceoff:

Get the puck to the shooter

In offensive-zone draws, the centre will usually try to get the puck back to the point or to a shooter in the slot. The easier play to

PP faceoffs

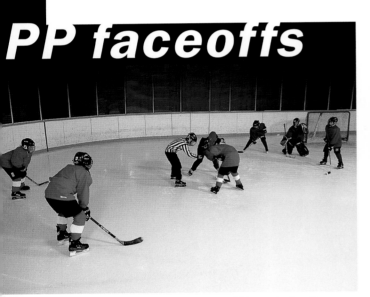

Every power-play faceoff is important. This centre has three options: the point, the slot, or the left-winger...

...The penalty-kill centre is quicker, so the power-play centre attacks his stick.

make is to the point, but a hard scoop directly backward can miss the target (the point's stickblade), forcing the power-play unit to gain entry to the zone again. A better plan is to block your opponent's stick, get control and move the puck to the shooter.

The moment you release the puck, go to the front of the net.

One-time the puck

If the faceoff is on the side that gives you a forehand shot on goal, think about doing just that. One-time the puck when it hits the ice. This works best if your opponent is holding his or her stick with the blade pointed toward the half-boards—the same side as yours. Often the goalie will cheat toward the middle and the shooter, leaving the short side open. Take a look. Go to the net for your own rebounds.

Move the puck ahead

Sometimes the best plan on a power-play faceoff in the offensive zone is to move the puck ahead, rather than drawing it back. This is a great idea if you have been losing most of your faceoffs. Let your teammates know what you have in mind. The trick is to get past your opponent and regain possession, usually in the corner. If you lose the draw and a penalty-kill defenseman has the puck, forecheck hard.

Be a solid tripod—by using your feet and stick. Watch the official's hand. The penalty-kill centre is swinging left to protect the puck...

... so the power-play centre attacks his stick. You can't win every faceoff, but you can avoid losing most of them.

PP faceoffs

PP faceoff tips

- Get your teammates set up the way you want them.
- Take a deep breath, and place your stickblade on the dot. Watch the referee's hand.
- If the faceoff is on your forehand side in the offensive zone, one-time it on the net. Go for the short side.
- Keep shots off the faceoff low. Think rebound.
- Don't always draw the puck back. Go forward sometimes. Keep them guessing.
- Never bug the ref. The referee gets the last word.

An underrated goalie, Guy Hebert can start Anaheim's speedy breakout with a quick pass to a defenseman to beat pressure from the forecheck.

Some goalies see the power play as vacation time. But there's a lot to do when your team has the advantage. You can be the one who triggers the power play, and the one who makes sure it ends safely. By staying in the game when your team has the manpower edge, you can help prevent a shorthanded goal. If you can pass the puck you might even get an assist. Here's what to work on.

Staying in the game

Be like John Vanbiesbrouck: Keep faith with your teammates by zeroing in on the puck—all the way to the other end of the rink. Most penalties called on your opponents will be in their zone. So be alert for easy-to-spot calls, like tripping, slashing or high-sticking. But remember: Do not call penalties for the referees. You know how refs hate that.

T I P

As a goalie, be the power-play trigger: Watch for penalties being called and skate to the bench.

Make the effort to stay in the game when your team is playing in the other end . . .

. . . If your teammate is the victim and the ref's arm is up, you're outta there . . .

. . . If your team has the puck and there's no whistle, make tracks for the bench.

PP goaltending

When you think you see a penalty, watch for the referee to raise his or her arm. When that happens, if your team is controlling the puck, hustle to the bench. Be ready to stop during the first few strides, just in case you are wrong, your opponents get control and no whistle is blown. Once you commit, skate hard.

Your teammates will usually be facing away from you, watching the play. So if nobody on the bench sees you coming, shout "Next centre!" You want the centre of the next line to replace you on the ice.

Watch for turnovers

On the power play, there is always plenty of warning when something goes wrong. It usually happens two zones away from you. Danger signs are cross-ice passes anywhere in the zone—but especially at the blueline—or a point man pinching or shooting into a checker's shinpads. Often you can see the turnover before it happens.

Turnovers on penalties often catch the power-play unit going the wrong way, so they often lead to breakaways or two-on-ones. But you do have time to get ready. Take a moment to be sure of your positioning. Commit to the shooter. Think of yourself as the equalizer.

PP goaltending

Power plays often give up great scoring chances. On two-on-one rushes, be high but not outside your crease. Take the shooter.

Point shots get blocked and turn into breakaways. Be ready. Make the shooter make the first move.

Take control

When play is in the offensive zone, set yourself up a little further out of the net than usual. Think of yourself as being in control of the space within the faceoff dots and the back-boards. You are in charge here. Talk to your teammates.

If you can handle the puck, you can save your teammates valuable seconds on the power play by stopping shootarounds and moving iced pucks up to your defensemen. Look around. Know what you intend to do with the puck before it gets to you. Then watch the puck into your glove or onto your stick.

The rules for goaltenders making passes are the same as for anyone else. Always make eye contact with the receiver before you pass. Look to see what side of the body the receiver's stick is on, and make a smooth, firm pass to that side. Sweep the puck, don't jerk it. Try to make the short, easy pass directly up the ice.

Making the big play

When you field a dump-in or an iced puck, chances are the penalty killers are changing. When you have the puck on your stick and feel no pressure, look for a teammate on the near side of the centre-ice line, on the opposite side of the ice from the benches. If that teammate is alone, make that pass.

T I P

When passing, aim for the tape on your receiver's stick. Follow through by pointing the end of your stickblade where you want the pass to go.

Make eye contact with the receiver before you pass the puck. Hit the tape.

The home-run pass: The penalty-kill unit is changing. Look for your teammate . . .

Let your teammates know the bad guy is back.

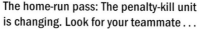

The sixth attacker

When it's over, it's over

Nothing gives a penalty-killing unit more of a lift than a scoring chance just as the penalty expires. You can help prevent that. Let your teammates know when there are 10 seconds left in the power play. Bang the blade of your stick on the ice.

When your teammates are in the offensive zone, the penalized player often leaves the box and returns to the ice behind their backs. Watch for the returning player to leave the box and warn the point man on that side, *by name,* if the other team is taking control of the puck.

Although a good power-play unit scores on one out of four penalties, a good penalty-killing unit can kill off nine out of 10 penalties. That means effective penalty killers are vital to any team. So if you want to be on the ice with the game on the line, be in on the penalty kill.

Often the most skilled offensive players are chosen for the power play, while the ones who always do the job go out when the team is down a player or two. There is more at stake on the penalty kill. And there is more enjoyment, not only because of a penalty-killing unit's higher success rate but because your teammates know you make a difference.

A good penalty-killing unit allows your team to play harder—*all* the time.

PENALTY

MARTIN RUCINSKY & JERE LEHTINEN ▶

KILLING

Coaches look for hockey smarts—the ability to read the play—in penalty killers. On a penalty kill, you need to know when to wait and when to attack the puck. You need to spot a turnover sooner than others do, and switch to offense while your opponents are still going the wrong way.

Next comes speed. It takes players who can skate well to make up for a missing player. Speed creates pressure on the power play. Speed cancels out mistakes. It turns the tables. Even when you don't have the puck yourself, your speed makes your opponents nervous. You can forecheck harder knowing you have the wheels to get back before the power-play unit gets to your zone.

Read and speed

Speed and positioning on the penalty kill are key. Here, Luke Holowaty sees Brooks Stillie, who is coming hard . . .

. . . they meet at the puck. Luke can't control it. Brooksie wins—this time.

What you need to know

There are two basic ways to kill penalties: passive and aggressive. Your coach will decide how your team should kill penalties, depending on your unit's ability to read-and-react, its speed and its puck skills. Passive means good positioning, taking few risks and waiting for the power play to make a mistake. Aggressive means attacking the power-play unit at every turn: forechecking its breakout, getting in the way through the neutral zone and standing up at your blueline.

Only after read and speed do we get to puck skills. For a smart player who can skate, the penalty-killing unit is the place to shine.

Defending in the offensive zone

Like all defensive aspects of hockey, a good penalty kill begins in the offensive zone, with forechecking. In any system, if you are the first forechecker into the zone you need to do three things:

1. Read how well the puck carrier is controlling the puck. If he or she is not handling the puck well, go hard to the puck.

2. Choose an angle on the puck carrier that the forechecker behind you can read. Take away one lane. If you are coming along the boards, seal off the boards and force a pass up the middle. Your teammate will read-and-react by moving into the open lane.

3. If the puck carrier retreats behind the net, **go** to the front of the net high in the slot area, and wait.

The power-play defenseman looks up-ice, but the forechecker is in the way. The defenseman then skates behind his own net to wait for help . . .

. . . while the forechecker waits out front, letting the defenseman waste seconds of his own power play.

Forechecking

Once the power play breaks out

Get back fast. Pick up your check in the neutral zone. If the wings are covered and the defense stands up at the blueline, many cross-ice passes will end up on defenders' sticks. Often the puck carrier (seeing the defense waiting) will slow down at your blueline and the others will go offside.

With both defensemen standing up at the blueline, easy entry into your defensive zone is denied. Remember: Your defense can only stand up at the blueline if they see that both pass-receiver forwards are covered by backcheckers. Otherwise they must back off to prevent those forwards from sneaking behind the defense.

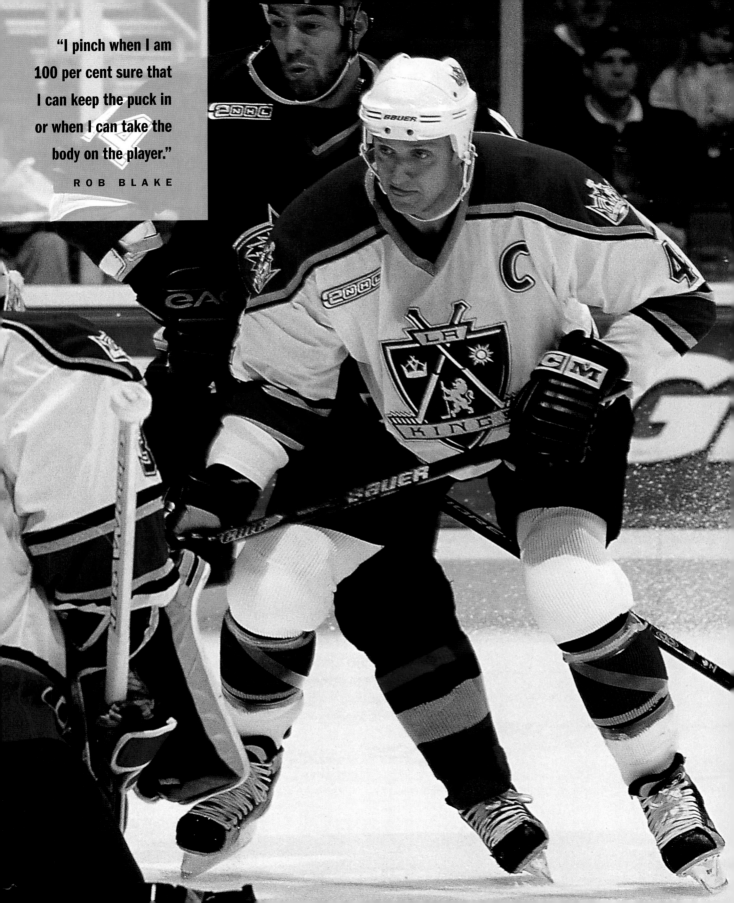

"I pinch when I am 100 per cent sure that I can keep the puck in or when I can take the body on the player."

ROB BLAKE

Once in a while, despite your best efforts, the power-play unit will set up in your zone with good puck possession. A good way to look at being on the penalty kill in your own zone is that you have your opponents where you want them. They are in your zone, where your goalie evens the numbers on a five-on-four penalty kill.

Think of yourself and your teammates as having an advantage. Your job is easy: Just keep the power play out of the shooting zone.

The walkout lanes

Think of yourself as checking two opponents: the ones on either side of you. You need to position yourself to take away the walkout lanes between you and the teammate on each side of you. Together, you and your teammates form a box. All four of you

N H L   T I P
"Stay out of any confusion down low. Be aware of where the opposing player is in front of the net and clear him out, while making sure that your goaltender can see the puck."
C H R I S   C H E L I O S

Good positioning has Brooksie covering two power-play forwards . . .

Brooksie reads the play, blocks the pass and goes after the puck carrier.

A quick poke-check does the trick.

In your zone

have your sticks on the ice, blocking the passing lanes your opponents want to move the puck through. Have your stick on the same side as the puck carrier's forehand.

We call it the "walkout lane" because the aim of the power-play unit is to get a player into your box—with the puck. A player inside your box with the puck is in the shooting zone. You and your penalty-killing unit are trying to cut off passes, clog the middle and prevent scoring chances.

Most of the time, the two forwards killing off a five-on-four penalty are checking the points, while the defensemen are in charge down low. But you are really covering two players. The reason for thinking you have two opponents (the ones on either side of you) to check is this: If one of them has the puck, his or her best play is a give-and-go, with the next player on either side breaking into the middle of your penalty-killing unit's box. That's a two-on-one, with you as the "one."

How do you defend a two-on-one? You stay between the two attacking players and block the pass. Anywhere near the net, defend against the pass and let your goalie take the shooter. As soon as an opponent gets inside the box, you and your teammates must back into the middle and down, toward your net. You remain in a box, but a smaller box.

Think two-on-one

Two penalty killers and the goalie are covering one side of the zone—even-up.

Even if the power-play unit gets the puck to the shooter closest to the net (which they have done here), everyone on the power play is covered. The goalie has the shooter.

When you get the puck

If you intercept the puck on the penalty kill, and you are not under pressure, hold onto it for a moment. Don't just hammer the puck up-ice. Are you being checked? If not, keep the puck. Look around. Is a teammate breaking out of the defensive zone? Is the power-play unit changing shifts? If you are confident of your puck-protection skills, carry the puck into your opponents' zone. Make the power-play unit come after you. Run the clock down. If you feel pressure you can still ice it.

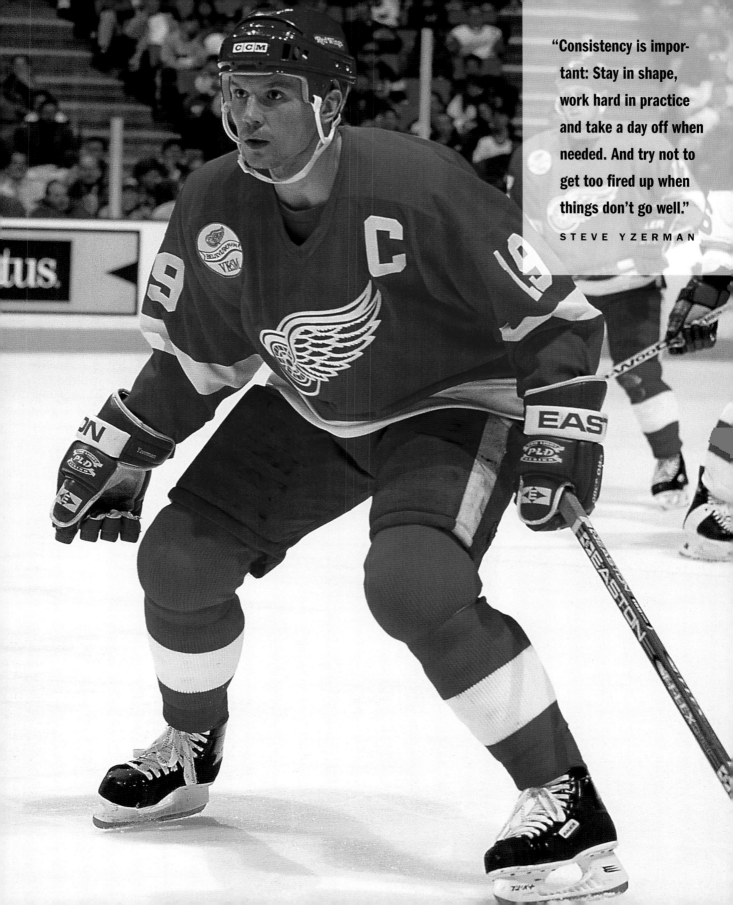

"Try to improve your defensive game with puck awareness and positioning, which is 90 per cent mental. It should seem like second nature to be where the puck is going to be."

CHRIS PRONGER

Blocking the shot

Blocking a point shot can hurt, but it can also get you a break-away. Line up with the puck, not the shooter's body. Stay square; never turn to the side. Expect the puck to bounce off your shin pads past the shooter. Skate hard past the shooter. Push the puck ahead of you, and carry it in the shooting position as soon as you reach the circles.

Never leave your feet, except when you are desperate. A shooter will often fake the shot to get you out of position. Hold your ground.

In-your-zone checklist

■ In the defensive zone, watch your check closely. Look for signs of weakness. Does he or she want the puck? Does your check receive the puck cleanly? If the answers are yes, back off and

Block the point shot with your shin pads and it will often bounce past the point man . . .

The goalie evens-up a two-on-one. The defenseman denies the pass, the goalie takes the shooter. It's really a two-on-two.

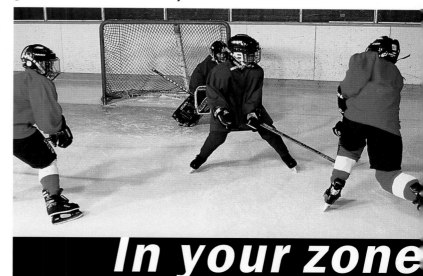

In your zone

position yourself to block passing lanes. If the answers are no (your check fumbles the puck or wants to get rid of it), attack.

■ Keep your stick active, placing it at the side of your body—blocking potential passing lanes.

■ Let the power-play unit move the puck around the outside of your zone for the entire two minutes if they want. Deny them one place: the mid-ice lane from the blueline in. A point shot from anywhere between the faceoff circles is a good scoring chance.

You can do it

Being two players down is not a death sentence. Usually the three players chosen to kill off a five-on-three are the team's best. They know that killing off a five-on-three can turn a game around. As for the power-play unit, it has too much of a good thing. It is expected to score; if its players can be kept off the scoreboard for even half a minute, they will be upset.

Killing any penalty gives a team a lift, but killing off a five-on-three changes a game's momentum almost like an unexpected goal does. Being chosen to be one of those three skaters on the ice is an honour, and it helps to know that the closer to your net the power play gets, the closer to even the numbers are.

Five-on-three

A five-on-three power play is not a death sentence. Stay in position and let the power-play unit give you the puck. A pass through the slot invites the penalty-killing unit to take the puck and go the other way.

Forecheck hard

It is always a good idea on a five-on-three to give the power-play unit a chance to hand you the puck. The single forward swings into the offensive zone, turns with the puck carrier and leaves the zone to pick up a wing. With that wing covered, the defense is now at even strength with the power-play forwards. Each can take one forward at the defense's blueline. If the forechecker picks up the power-play unit's centre, the same matchups are there.

Remember: If the power-play unit dumps the puck, the defense has to hustle back. If the defense gets there first and clears the puck, the power play has to start out again.

When the other team has control of the puck in your zone, there are three ways to play the triangle in a five-on-three power play.

Standard triangle: The most common triangle puts the forward at the apex, in the slot, with the defensemen where they would be in a four-player box: just inside the faceoff circles, about even with the dots. The forward covers the high slot and the points. When there isn't much pressure on them, the points will often move in. When that happens, look for the defense-to-defense pass that can be deflected or intercepted.

Rotating triangle: The forward at the point of the triangle tries to take away the defense-to-defense pass with his stick in the lane. In case that pass gets across, the weak-side defender, positioned

Close to the net, the three penalty killers have the advantage. The closer to the net, the more important the goalie becomes.

The forward on this five-on-three is blocking the passing lane to the uncovered player.

Playing the triangle

close to the slot, must move out to defend against a point shot. The forward then drops back to take a position low on the triangle. This way the penalty-killing unit keeps pressure on the puck and lends support close to its own net.

Sliding triangle: Not every five-on-three has to be killed by two defensemen and one forward. A triangle with a single defenseman and two forwards works just as well to keep pressure on the points. The defenseman moves in front of his or her net from post-to-post, depending on what side the puck is on. The forwards move in and out: the forward on the strong-side out, the weak-side forward in, keeping an eye on the power-play forwards down low.

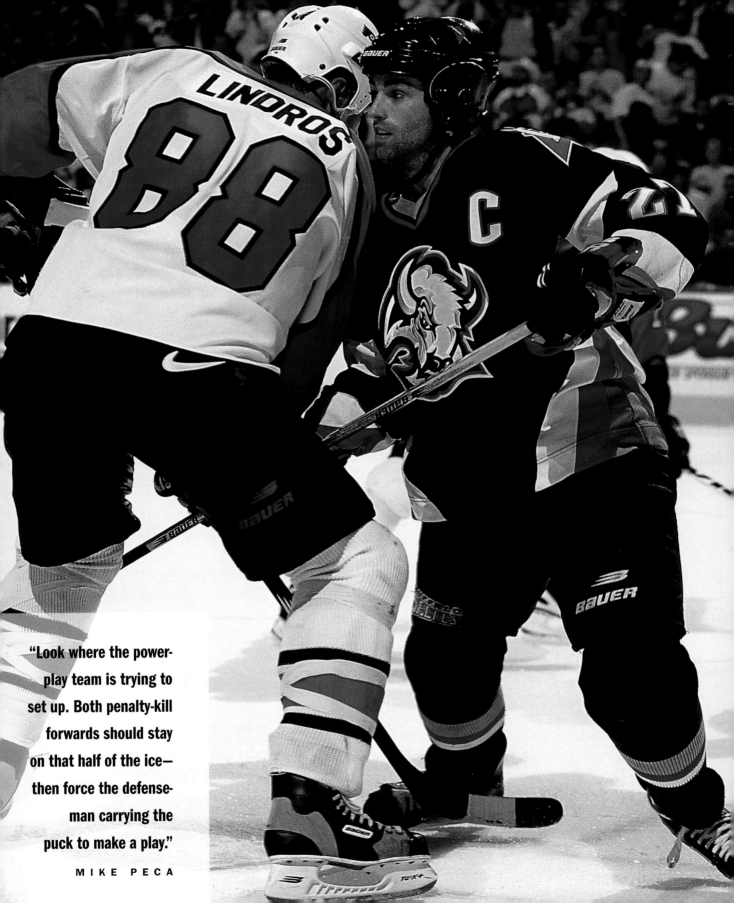

"Look where the power-play team is trying to set up. Both penalty-kill forwards should stay on that half of the ice—then force the defense-man carrying the puck to make a play."

MIKE PECA

Stay confident

When you are outnumbered, every faceoff has a life-or-death feel to it. But winning faceoffs cleanly on the penalty kill is extra-important—especially in your own zone. There are two reasons. First, a lost faceoff in your own zone often leads to a close-in scoring chance for the power play. Second, penalty killers get tired quickly, and often the only way to get a change is to freeze the puck—which means another faceoff in your own zone.

Study your opponent

Some coaches will allow you to watch your opposing centre on the first few faceoffs of the game, or on early draws at centre ice, to see how your opponent likes to take them. Also, watch faceoffs from the bench to see how the officials handle the puck.

Before you put your stick down, have a plan. Be prepared for anything. Watch the ref's hand.

The red power-play centre is winning the faceoff by reacting faster. The blue centre must block his opponent's way to the net.

PK faceoffs

Take charge

Faceoffs are one time when the centre is in charge on the ice. On a defensive-zone faceoff, make sure your teammates are where you want them to be. Never go to the dot without checking your teammates. Finally, check your goalie. Once you put your stick down, take a deep breath to relax and concentrate. Look at the puck in the official's hand out of the corner of your eye.

And remember: Whether you win or lose a faceoff, you can always prevent your opposing centre from going to the net.

Read-and-react

All faceoffs are different, even on a penalty kill. How you need to handle a penalty-kill faceoff each time depends on how you have been doing against your opponent so far, where the faceoff was called and how you usually win them. In your own zone, it is often more important not to lose faceoffs than to win them cleanly. Go for your opponent's stick.

PK faceoff tips

- The best penalty-kill faceoff result is a clean draw back to the corner, away from the net. The defenseman can ice the puck or start a breakout by moving it to you, his or her partner, or up the boards. Use the reverse lower-hand grip and draw straight back.

PK faceoffs

The power-play centre attacks the penalty-kill centre's stick. The puck is up for grabs...

...so the penalty-kill centre skates into his opponent, pushing him off the puck. A teammate has control of the puck and can waste time or ice it.

T I P
If your opponent attacks your stick, use your leg on that side to protect it.

- One way not to lose an important faceoff is to rotate your leg on your opponent's forehand side around the puck to protect it. Lean into your opponent, and use your skateblade to poke the puck back. Another way to neutralize your opponent is to lift his or her stick and kick the puck back.
- When your opponent lines up on his or her forehand and has a direct shot on net, you are in a defensive position. Attack your opponent's shaft above the blade or jam the blade itself. Try to stay between your opposing centre and your team's net, in case the shot gets through and there's a rebound.

"Winning a power-play faceoff in the offensive zone gives a team more time to set up, pass the puck and get the best possible scoring chance."

DOUG WEIGHT

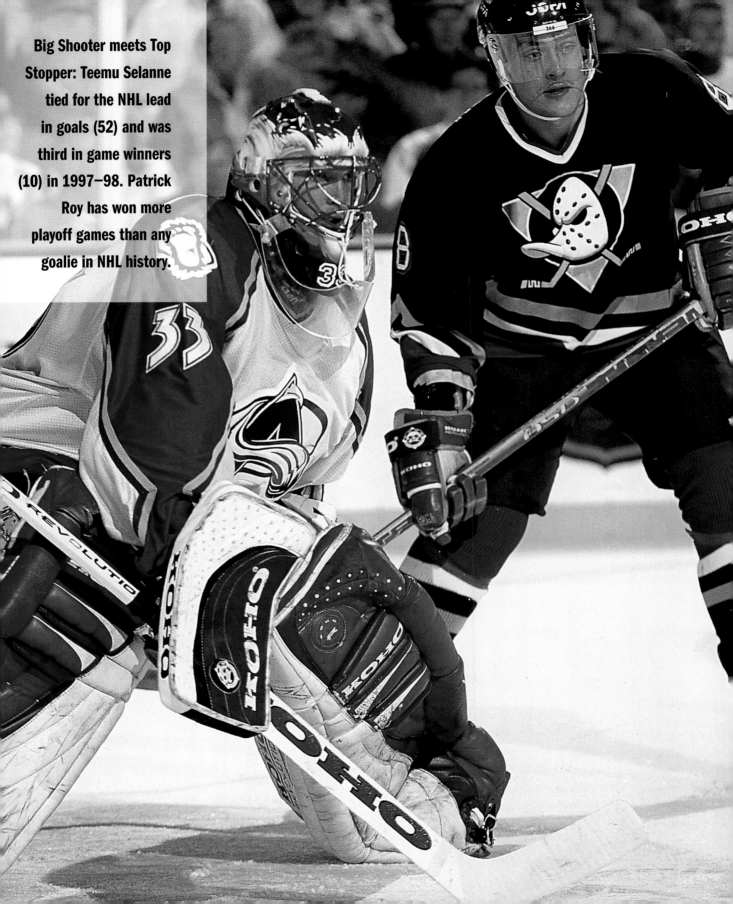

Big Shooter meets Top Stopper: Teemu Selanne tied for the NHL lead in goals (52) and was third in game winners (10) in 1997–98. Patrick Roy has won more playoff games than any goalie in NHL history.

Be prepared

As a goalie, nobody has to tell you what to do when your team is shorthanded. This is the time for you to step up and be the equalizer. A smart goalie can improve the penalty-killing unit's chances of holding the fort when it's surrounded and outnumbered.

You have to use all the tricks in your bag on a penalty kill. Save your energy. Stay on your feet. Be ready for rebounds. Don't give up on screen shots—in fact, expect them. Get your head down and look through the legs in front.

Most important, never blame anyone else when the other guys score. It takes at least two mistakes—one of them yours—to add up to a goal. The penalty-killing unit works hard in front of you, so be its biggest backer.

> **T I P**
> Think of penalties as your chance to shine. Welcome the puck into your zone. Let it come to you.

Never use screens as an excuse. Keep your eyeballs on the puck. You can see better through legs than bodies.

Tory Malinoski helps his penalty killers by turning low shots into the corners—avoiding costly rebounds.

PK goaltending

Penalties take a lot out of goaltenders; the intensity that penalties require is why working out pays off. Mike Richter runs around the Madison Square Garden ice-level hallway before every home game. Be like Mike.

Don't overreact

Remember: Two or five minutes can be an eternity. So don't overreact. Take it one shot at a time. Don't come out as far on point shots as you would at other times—if the shot goes wide it can be tipped in by the low forward behind you.

How to play it

Once play gets close to your net, stay between the posts and play the shooter as always, but expect the pass. You can make the shooter pass by being in position and moving sideways. The more passes the better. Sooner or later the power-play unit will give your team the puck. If you are in position, often you won't have to make the save because the shooter won't take the shot.

Turn aside low shots. Be happy when the points shoot high. Once the puck is in your glove you can relax.

Take every break you can get. Have a drink of water during each stop in play. And, while you're doing that, tell yourself that the most important save is the next one. Every chance you get, any time you have doubts, freeze the puck. It doesn't just stop the play, it also takes at least a couple of seconds off the clock when the referee hesitates to blow the whistle.

PK goaltending

Point shots that can be seen and aren't deflected don't often score. Tory's penalty-kill teammates are keeping the power play out of his way...

... but no penalty-killing unit is perfect. Sometimes goalies have to make big saves.

T I P

Call "Time!" if you are not ready for a faceoff. Do it before the linesman is set to drop the puck.

Be alive on faceoffs

If part of your penalty-killing plan is to break up the penalty by getting faceoffs, make sure they don't backfire. If you are facing the centre's forehand shot, watch for it. Most times, the centre will try to get the puck to the shooter in the slot. Most shots from there are screened. Be prepared for the screen shot. Don't ever make it an excuse.

Martin Brodeur might be the best all-around goalie in hockey, with a GAA under 2.30 four years in a row. Adept with his stick around the net, he was the first goalie to score a playoff goal, in 1997.

The key to the Montreal Canadiens' hopes for a return to greatness lies with Jeff Hackett, winner of about 20 games for every year he's been a starter—always with low-scoring teams.

Handle the puck

Stopping the puck behind the net on shootarounds is extra-important on the penalty kill. Learn to expect shootarounds if your penalty-killing unit is clogging up the blueline. Make the stop and then look to see who's coming. It's a plus for your team if you can flip the puck around the boards or out of the zone. But don't try it in a game until you know you can do it every time.

When you have the puck in your glove and an unchecked team-mate is on his or her way, set the puck down for an easy pickup.

Stay in touch with your teammates

Some goalies go into a shell under pressure. But you are the only one on your team who can see most of the zone. Let the defense know when there's an unchecked opponent nearby. Often, the low

N H L T I P
"As the goalie on the penalty kill, I try to communicate with the other players on the ice. I let them know whether they have time or if there's pressure. Being vocal is very important."
R O N   T U G N U T T

Even the best power plays don't often get chances like this. Tory moves across with the shooter.

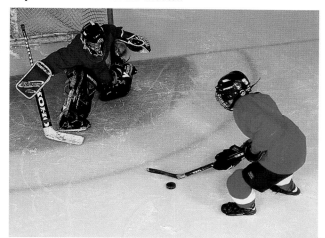

This two-on-one, like all two-on-ones, is actually a two-on-two. The second defender is the goalie. Tory plays the shooter.

PK goaltending

forward on the power play lurks beside the weak-side post. Tell your defenseman. As the penalty winds down to the last 30 seconds, let your penalty-killing unit know how much time is left. Often the defense will turn their backs on checkers to race for the puck. If there's a checker right behind, yell "Man on you!"

If there are two opposing checkers along the boards, shout "Two to beat!" When your teammate gets control of the puck and an opponent is coming from behind, yell "Behind you!" Try to keep your instructions to two or three words.

Credits

Photography

Photography by Stefan Schulhof/Schulhof Photography, except as indicated below:

Photos by Bruce Bennett Studios:
Front cover, back cover & title page spread (Peter Forsberg,
    Martin Rucinsky & Jere Lehtinen), p. 1 (background), p. 16 (background),
    p. 17, p. 36 (background), p. 37, p. 56, p. 59: Bruce Bennett
Back cover & title page spread (Pavel Bure), p. 4, p. 21, p. 24, p. 48,
    p. 51: Jim McIsaac
Back cover & title page spread (Patrick Roy & Teemu Selanne), p. 10,
    p. 13, p. 44, p. 52: John Giamundo
Back cover & title page spread (Mark Recchi), p. 7, p. 55:
    Jim Leary
Back cover & title page spread (Jaromir Jagr), p. 8 (background),
    p. 9: Dennis Clark
p. 23: Henry DiRocco
p. 29: John Russell
p. 32, p. 60: Andre Pichette
p. 40: Scott Levy
p. 43: Wen Roberts

Photo of Marc Crawford on p. 5 by Jeff Vinnick, provided courtesy of the Vancouver Canucks

NHL player quotes

All NHL player tips were given by the players to the authors for the purposes of this book, except as indicated below:

p. 21 (Pavel Bure tip): McKenzie, Bob. "Scoring Machine." *The Hockey News* 53, no. 20 (2000): 10–11.

p. 23 (Paul Kariya tip): Plunkett, Bill. "NHL Team Reports." *The Hockey News* 53, no. 20 (2000): 17.

p. 49 (Doug Gilmour tip): Wheatley, Tom. "Art of the Draw." *Beckett Hockey Monthly* 5, no. 3 (1994): 62–64.

p. 60 (Teemu Selanne tip): Duhatschek, Eric. "Speed Demon." *The Calgary Herald* (February 4, 1998) / Web site.

Other books in this award-winning series:

Hockey the NHL Way: The Basics
Hockey the NHL Way: Goal Scoring
Hockey the NHL Way: Goaltending
Hockey the NHL Way: Win with Defense

"Speed is important on the power play—in your team's breakout, in gaining the attacking zone and in keeping possession of the puck in the opposition's end."

JEREMY ROENICK

"You have to be able to
handle the puck at top
speed. You also have to
play smart and try to
read the game. Making
the right decisions
is the most important
part in hockey."

TEEMU SELANNE